How to Draw
CUTE
WOODLAND
FRIENDS

This book belongs to:

....

....

How to Draw
CUTE
WOODLAND
FRIENDS

Angela Nguyen

union
square
kids

NEW YORK

union
square
kids
NEW YORK

UNION SQUARE KIDS and the distinctive
Union Square Kids logo are trademarks of
Union Square & Co.

Union Square & Co., LLC, is a subsidiary
of Sterling Publishing Co., Inc.

© 2023 Quarto Publishing plc

First Union Square Kids edition published in 2023

ISBN 978-1-4549-5052-3
ISBN: 978-1-4549-5053-0 (e-book)

For information about custom editions, special sales,
and premium purchases, please contact
specialsales@unionsquareandco.com.

Printed in China

2 4 6 8 10 9 7 5 3 1

06/23

unionsquareandco.com

MIX
Paper | Supporting
responsible forestry
FSC® C016973

CONTENTS

Hi there, my name is Angela!

I'm the author of this book! I'm an artist who specializes in drawing cute stuff, and turning everything and anything cute. I'll show you how throughout each page. Or, if you just want an adorable art book, that's OK too.

Woodland stuff has a special place in my heart because I love nature; I live in the Pacific Northwest of the United States, known for its abundance of trees, mountains, and water. There's also lots of animals, people, foods, and plants that are woodland themed, which you will find in this book. Join me on this woodland journey to draw really cute things!

Yours truly,

ANGELA NGUYEN

Chapter one

GETTING STARTED

You don't need special tools, materials, or skills to draw your woodland world. Grab your pens and paper, then learn how to give your drawings cute appeal! You can also have some fun creating the scenery for your woodland folk and creatures.

TOOLS AND SURFACES

There are many types of tools you can use to draw and color cute woodland creatures. These are some of the tools that I love to use.

The pencil is a go-to!

CRAYONS

If you're going to be doing a lot of coloring, crayons can be a fun tool to play with. They make interesting textures and thick strokes.

PENCILS

Pencils are ideal for sketching and creating fun textures. Pencil marks are also easy to erase.

If you want to keep all your drawings together, you could use a sketchbook, or a simple notebook will do.

Funky erasers

How cute is this frog pencil topper?

Try not to drop colored pencils because the lead inside will break.

SURFACES

You don't need special paper; any kind of drawing surface is just fine.

You can pick up any piece of paper and draw a creature on it.

Look at this woodland fox pencil topper!

MARKERS

Markers can be a bit risky because they are ink-heavy, so test them out first. I have some markers in my office that are light and create beautiful thick strokes.

Thick markers define lines.

PENS

These are my favorite! Pens are great when you want a thin stroke. You can get precise markings, perfect facial expressions, or pattern details.

MAKING THEM CUTE

These are the three guidelines that I use to turn any drawing into a cute masterpiece. Follow these steps to make your drawings super adorable too!

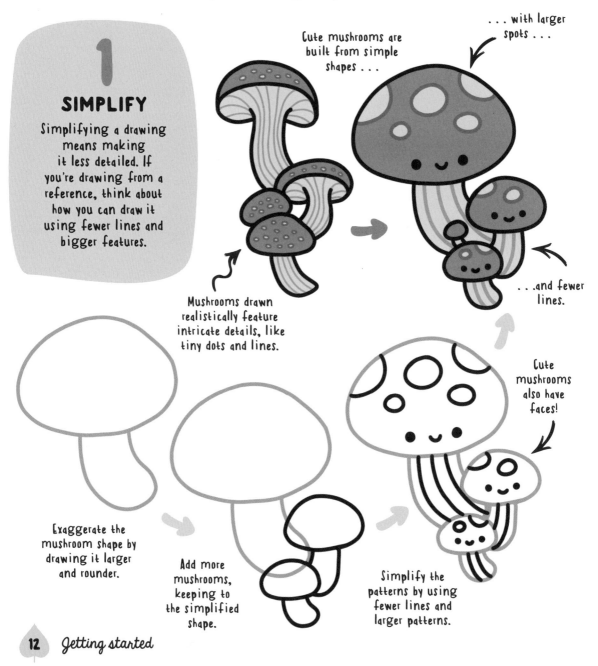

1

SIMPLIFY

Simplifying a drawing means making it less detailed. If you're drawing from a reference, think about how you can draw it using fewer lines and bigger features.

Cute mushrooms are built from simple shapes . . .

. . . with larger spots . . .

. . . and fewer lines.

Mushrooms drawn realistically feature intricate details, like tiny dots and lines.

Cute mushrooms also have faces!

Exaggerate the mushroom shape by drawing it larger and rounder.

Add more mushrooms, keeping to the simplified shape.

Simplify the patterns by using fewer lines and larger patterns.

2
ROUNDED SHAPES

Another way to simplify your drawings and make them cuter, is to use plenty of rounded, curved shapes, rather than sharp, pointy shapes.

When drawing a realistic wolf, the fur is usually depicted using sharp lines and points.

The fur details on the cute wolf are rounded, and so are the ears, tail, and legs.

These are quite realistic frog colors . . .

3
COLOR CHOICE

Colors indicate at first glance how bright and friendly your character is. Use pastel or lighter colors instead of dark, dull colors.

. . . but lighter colors look cuter.

BASIC SHAPES

The world is full of amazing things that you can draw using just a few basic shapes. Each shape can be drawn longer, skinnier, fatter, larger, or smaller to create other shapes.

Ovals and circles

Squares and rectangles

Triangles

Jelly beans

Gumdrops

See how the shapes combine to create a character.

Triangle ears

Circle head

Jelly bean body

Rectangle limbs

Triangle tail

Circle wings

Jelly bean body

PATTERNS

Patterns are usually repeating shapes, and you can use them to add the finishing touches to your characters, clothes, or accessories.

One way to make patterns is to repeatedly draw the same shape.

Changing the angle or the color of the shape is an easy way to make your pattern look more stylish.

It is not essential, but you might want to space your shape out evenly to make your pattern. Stagger them so that the ones below and above are in between your first row.

You can combine lots of patterns, like on this cozy quilt.

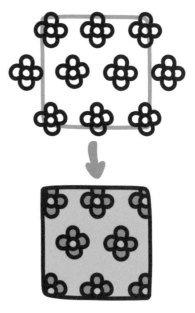

Put patterns on things like furniture or clothes.

Check out this patterned shirt.

SCENERY

The scenery you use in your drawings tells the story of where your character is from, how they live, and what they are up to right now!

Mountain lands are high up, and so closer to the clouds. Forests of evergreens are usual on mountainsides, and there is often snow on the mountaintops. There's also lots of fresh water in mountain environments.

On meadows and hillsides the main features are grass and flowers. This environment is perfect for animals that graze and bugs that pollinate flowers.

In a forest scene there will be lots of trees to frame the drawing. You can add bushes under the trees and piles of leaves on the ground.

Rivers and lakes are bodies of water surrounded by land. The land around the water is usually green and fertile.

Chapter two

WOODLAND FOLK

Drawing cute people requires features to distinguish them, and accessories and clothes to decorate them. In this chapter, I'll show you how to bring all sorts of characters to life!

PEOPLE BASICS

PROPORTIONS

Two-and-a-half circles is the perfect proportion for cute characters. The top circle is the head. The body takes up roughly three-quarters of the middle circle, and the legs reach from the bottom of the body to the base line.

Add hair and facial features . . .   . . . and clothes and finishing touches.

BODY SHAPES

Use the same proportion guidelines to draw different body shapes!

This character has an oval head with a narrow body and slim limbs.

Try square shapes with wide limbs.

You can even draw a triangular body.

DIRECTIONS

Draw a cross on your character's face. As you draw them turning in different directions, keep the eyes the same distance apart on the horizontal line, and the nose and mouth the same distance below on the vertical line.

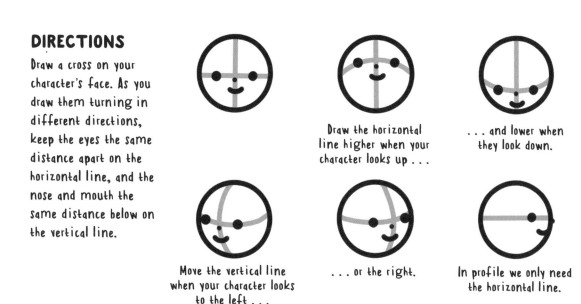

Draw the horizontal line higher when your character looks up . . .

. . . and lower when they look down.

Move the vertical line when your character looks to the left . . .

. . . or the right.

In profile we only need the horizontal line.

HAIRSTYLES

There are many hairstyles to choose from, so think about your character's personality and lifestyle to help you choose. These are just some examples you could try.

Which one is your favorite?

POSES

Once you've mastered the basic principles of body proportions, shapes, and directions, you can start to explore poses for your characters.

Here is a front-facing character with a gumdrop body shape.

By changing the shapes of the body and limbs in small ways, you can create different poses.

Use the cross on the face to help you understand the direction your character is facing.

The head shape is a circle, even when it faces in different directions.

When the legs are lifted like this, it makes the person look like they are floating.

Drawing the head away from the gumdrop body makes the pose lean forward.

When the hands are together, you can add items for your character to hold.

Try drawing people together and see how they can interact with one another, such as holding hands, taking a stroll, or exploring woodlands together.

EXPRESSIONS

Use facial expressions to show how your character is feeling, and bring them to life. What kind of mood are your woodland friends in today?

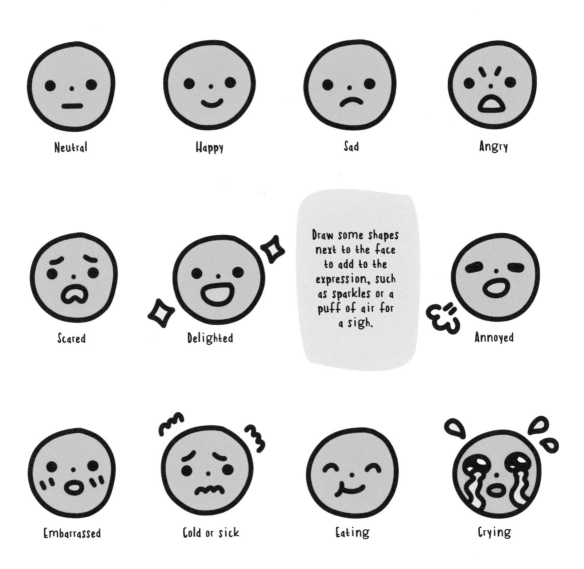

Neutral

Happy

Sad

Angry

Scared

Delighted

Draw some shapes next to the face to add to the expression, such as sparkles or a puff of air for a sigh.

Annoyed

Embarrassed

Cold or sick

Eating

Crying

Smirky

Loving

Even animal characters can have fun expressions! Try some of these.

Excited

Dizzy

Shocked

Laughing

Sassy

Winking

One of my favorite expressions is the winking face. It's cute and simple!

Worried

Tired

CLOTHES

When it comes to dressing your woodland folk, there are so many choices. Remember to think about accessories as well as the main outfit, to make sure your character looks the part.

Applying clothes

Start with your character's basic shape of head, body, and limbs.

Add the main outfit, such as pants or a skirt, and a top.

Don't forget the details, such as buttons, collars, pockets, zippers, cuffs, etc.

Finish by choosing your character's color scheme. This guy is very tidy.

Tops

Long, puffy sleeves have a cuff at the wrist.

Add patterns to your clothes.

This short-sleeved top has a wide body and a collar detail.

Overalls are practical for woodland folk.

Use wavy lines to give a dress some frilly details.

An apron could be a useful piece of clothing for an artist.

Bottoms

These shorts are really puffy, with frilly cuffs.

A plaid pattern works well on a skirt.

These shorts have cuffs, pockets, and a zipper.

Pleat lines look good on a long skirt.

You might want to add a waistband feature to your pants, shorts, or skirts.

Explore your own fashion ideas. This cool skirt is tied at the waist.

Accessories

Why wear boring socks? Add playful patterns to your accessories.

This hat is perfectly forest themed, with its mushroom shape and pattern.

Some woodland folk will need shoes, or even sturdy boots like these.

If your character is picking fruit, they'll need a basket.

If your character is collecting nuts, then an acorn bag may be just the thing to hold them in.

Hats are fun accessories, as are other types of headdress, like this flower crown.

WOODLAND CREATORS

Creators like artists, florists, musicians, bakers, and more, are inspired by the world around them, and forest life is a never-ending source of inspiration.

Draw the artist's painting pose, with brush in hand.

Draw an oval covering the front arm for the paint palette. Add a hairstyle and clothes.

Draw an angled rectangle for the canvas . . .

. . . and add the outline of the easel.

Florist

Draw the pose and add long, wavy hair.

Add a floaty dress, lines for shoes, a flower crown, and flowers in her hair.

Give the florist a basket and fill it with blooms.

Musician

This character has an oval head.

A guitar has an avocado shape, with straight lines coming out at the thin end.

Give your musician a mushroom hat!

Draw hands on top of the guitar.

Baker

This baker is in a rush! Draw them in a running pose.

Add the hair, a neckerchief, a basket to fill with bread, and a rolling pin.

Reader

A reader is also a type of creator! They use their imagination and are inspired by the stories they read.

WITCHES

Witches are powerful beings who can perform magic. They love animals and studying new spells, and have cool accessories like crystal balls, wands, and broomsticks.

Start with the base of the body and a powerful facial expression.

Make the dress flare out and the arms wrap in front of the body.

Make the hair spiky like fire.

Make her setting spiky too.

— Casting a spell —

Draw this cute pose with one circle hand holding the wand . . .

. . . while the other hand points outward.

Add a triangle hat . . .

. . . and a big dress.

Draw a broomstick and sit your witch on it, with crossed legs.

The direction lines on the face really help with the pose.

Draw a rounded triangle to start the brush end.

Add in the details, including the cat.

When a witch leans forward, her cape flies backward. This character has a rabbit for a companion.

Studying spells

This witch is looking downward, so use your direction lines.

Add some floating books too.

Draw the cape flared outward on both sides of the body. The hands are circles, ready to hold a book.

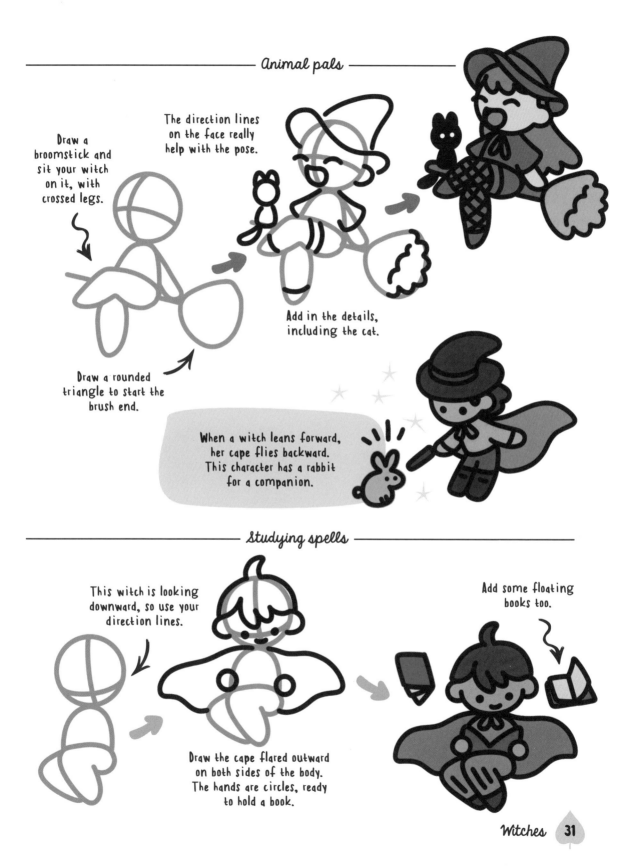

DRYADS

Dryads are mythical forest-dwelling beings. They are infused into the forest itself, which is why they have treelike bodies.

Draw one arm up and the other down.

Add lines to show that the body is made of wood.

Give your dryad long hair and branches on top of their head, like antlers.

--- Branch arms ---

Give this dryad a giant branch arm! Start with a basic arm shape . . .

. . . then, add long, branchlike fingers.

Trunk legs

Start with a seated pose.

Add a tree trunk coming out from the legs.

Add bark lines to the trunk.

Make the hair bushy with leaves.

Root arms

Draw the long arms like rectangular wings to start.

Another fun way to draw dryad limbs is as roots. Roots can intertwine with one another and make fun shapes.

Draw the roots inside and around the rectangle bases.

Notice the cute leafy pigtails.

GNOMES

These small woodland creatures bring good luck if you spot one. Because they are tiny and good at hiding, it is particularly difficult to find them! Try checking under a leaf.

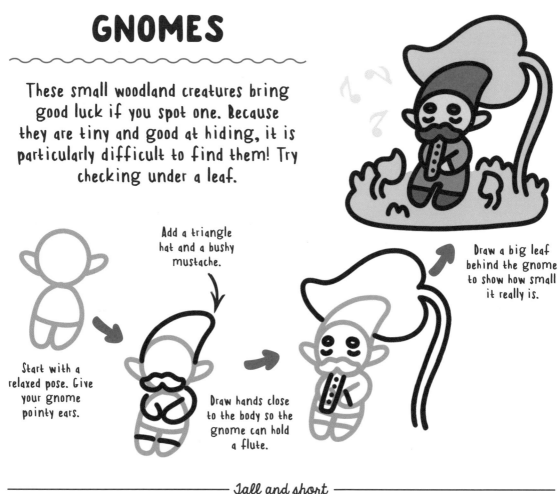

Add a triangle hat and a bushy mustache.

Draw a big leaf behind the gnome to show how small it really is.

Start with a relaxed pose. Give your gnome pointy ears.

Draw hands close to the body so the gnome can hold a flute.

Tall and short

You can use the people size guide (see page 20) to proportion your gnomes, or you can make smaller gnomes by using one less circle.

Add a circle nose near the top of the oval and a big triangular hat.

The base of this gnome is simply a wide oval with small, stubby limbs.

Draw a beard around the bottom of the oval.

Give your gnome a cute flower to hold.

Change the position of the hands and add lines around your character to change its expression without a face! This gnome is jumping for joy!

Snail ride

Draw a sitting gnome with the classic triangle hat.

Add a beard and eyes.

Draw a snail (see pages 68–69) for your gnome to ride on.

Gnomes 35

TROLLS

Trolls are incredibly strong, and like to roam from forest to mountain exploring caves and rocky areas.

The ears and nose are also oval-shaped.

The body is a wide oval with a small circular head and chubby limbs.

Give your troll forest-inspired clothing and accessories.

Scruffy troll

Draw a seated base with the legs close to the body.

Use wavy lines to give your troll lots of foliage hair and detailing.

Add leaves sticking out all over the troll.

Animal lover

To make limbs point toward you, draw them as circles.

The horns and ears are rounded triangles.

Draw little birds around your animal-loving troll!

Sad troll

Draw fallen tears on the outfit too.

This troll's body is a circle rather than an oval.

Continue with a worried face and a frilly outfit.

Draw tears on the face and coming out at the sides.

Traveling stick

Draw one arm as a circle while the other arm points out and back.

Draw wrapped clothes and rugged pants using triangles.

Give the troll a traveling stick with a bundle of their possessions tied at the end.

FAIRIES

Fairies are tiny and love their natural habitats. To show how small they are, make sure to draw big flowers or foliage around them.

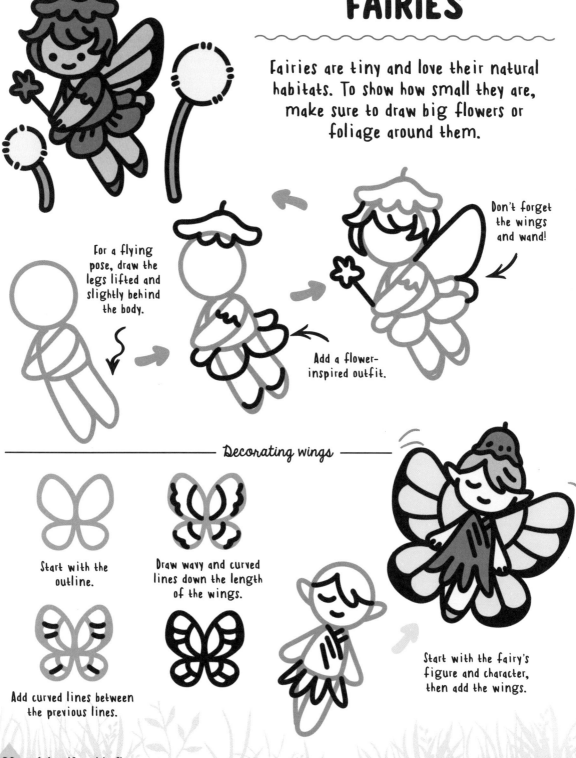

For a flying pose, draw the legs lifted and slightly behind the body.

Add a flower-inspired outfit.

Don't forget the wings and wand!

Decorating wings

Start with the outline.

Draw wavy and curved lines down the length of the wings.

Add curved lines between the previous lines.

Start with the fairy's figure and character, then add the wings.

Sitting on a flower

Position your fairy sitting on a curved line. Draw a large circle at the end of the line.

Draw petals inside the circle.

Make a leafy collar for a cool outfit!

Holding a mushroom

Draw a line across the body, then a circle and a curved triangle at the end of the line.

Curve the front arm so it holds the mushroom.

Flower hat

Add petal shapes on top of the head.

Add on wings to the back. They are similar in shape to the petals!

PLANT PEOPLE

Plant people are infused with the shapes, colors, and patterns of plants. Check out these examples and have a go at inventing your own plant people!

Start with a seated pose.

Give this character big bushy hair and bush-shaped clothing.

Add flowers and extra leaves in the hair.

sapling person

Draw a person with a surprised look!

For the hair, draw spiky triangles. Add teardrop shapes for the leaves on top.

Give this character a backpack, scarf, and a walking stick.

Acorn person

This acorn person is leaping from tree to tree, like a squirrel.

Add an acorn hat and acorn patterns on the clothes.

Draw in jumping lines and a squirrel friend too!

Leaf hair

The trick with drawing leaves as hair is to start with a line.

Then add leaves to the line until you fill it completely.

Vine hair

Add more lines and join them to create the vines.

Add some leaves

Long, curving vines make dynamic hairstyles. The vines can twist and turn in all directions.

Draw the pose and add curved lines from the crown of the head all the way past the feet.

FLOWER PEOPLE

There are so many flowers out there, so there are infinite possibilities for creating flower characters! You can make the face, outfit, or pose flower-inspired!

Begin with the base.

Draw flower petals around the head.

Draw wavy lines inside the petals to create a new frilly shape.

Give the petals a bright color and make the body green, like a stem.

Petal hat and outfit

For this character, the petals wrap around the face.

Draw petals around the body too, like a skirt.

Finish up by adding a stem on top of the flower hat.

Flower bud

The base of this pose is a circle instead of a gumdrop.

Draw lines on the circle body to turn it into a flower bud. Draw leaves to the side of the bud and a stem hat.

Rose collar

Draw a circle around the head.

Draw the petals inside the circle so they surround the head.

The arms are leaves.

Fuzzy pollen

After making the base, draw petals around the neck.

Make the head fuzzy and draw a cute face!

CAT PEOPLE

Cat people have the characteristics and personality traits of cats. They like to meet new people and jump up and down in joy when they can hang out with friends.

To make a thumbs-up pose, draw a small circle on top of the paw circle.

Draw the base of a person with a winky face. The front paw is a circle.

Add on the hair and triangular ears. The clothes are simple lines.

Draw me with arms up and a happy face, jumping for joy!

I drew inspiration from a surprised cat's pose for this drawing. The arms point down and the tail points up.

Sleepy kitty

For this pose, draw the back legs close to the body.

Draw the front legs closer to the body too.

Notice how the eyes slant downward.

WATER SPRITES

Water sprites live near freshwater lakes because they enjoy swimming every day. Use cool pastel colors so they look watery.

Notice that the shapes of the body and limbs are rounded.

Even the hair and top fin are rounded. Add lines on the limbs to make fin patterns.

The tail is like a curved limb. Don't forget to add the same fin patterns there too!

Floating away

In this pose, the limbs are wavy, like water.

Draw the fin lines in the same wavy direction as the limbs.

Finish with wavy lines behind the character to show that they are swimming or walking.

DEER PEOPLE

Notable qualities of deer people are their long antlers and big ears. The antlers point upward while the ears point outward!

Start with the base of a person. Then add arms and antlers.

Draw in the hair, ears, tail, and details for the clothes.

Deer move in many ways, including prancing and galloping. This deer person is trotting along.

Jumping pose

Try drawing this jumping pose!

Add antlers, ears, and clothes.

Use different shades of brown to color your drawing.

Add direction lines to emphasize the jump.

BIRD PEOPLE

Bird people are fun to draw because of their giant wings! The wings can be used to express the character's feelings and make dynamic poses.

Start the wings as jelly beans. The wing closest to you should look bigger than the one behind.

Draw feathers inside the wings and as details around the character.

With the wings open or upward, your bird person will look friendly and welcoming. Draw the wings covering the body if your bird person is worried or afraid.

Sassy bird

In this fun pose, one wing is down while the other is up.

This is a sassy pose, so give your character a sassy expression too.

Chapter three

FOREST CREATURES

A whole host of woodland creatures awaits—
birds, bears, bugs, and more, as well as new
creatures that have popped straight out of
my imagination!

FOXES

Foxes are playful creatures with triangle ears and bushy tails. They like to pounce when they are playing and curl up into cozy balls when they're napping.

Add the face, and paws, and color it in.

Start with a circle and a jelly bean body. Add the tail pointing upward.

Draw the rounded snout, ears, and limbs. Add a zigzag line to the tail.

Fox face

Begin with a circle.

Add four soft triangles to create the ears and mouth.

Color the fox orange and add white fur details.

Foxes have triangular faces and ears so keep that in mind when you draw them from different angles.

A foxy bouquet

Add the flowers.

Start with an oval and add circle paws and triangle ears.

Create the bouquet with an upside-down triangle.

Add the foliage, face, and paw details, and color it in!

Jumping fox

Add zigzag lines to show the white-tipped tail (the brush).

Start with a circle, oval, and a jelly bean tail.

Add the snout, ears, and limbs for a pouncing pose.

Add the details, including white dots for the eyebrows and ears.

RABBITS

Woodland rabbits are adorable creatures that love to play together. They sometimes even leave the forest to steal carrots from nearby fields.

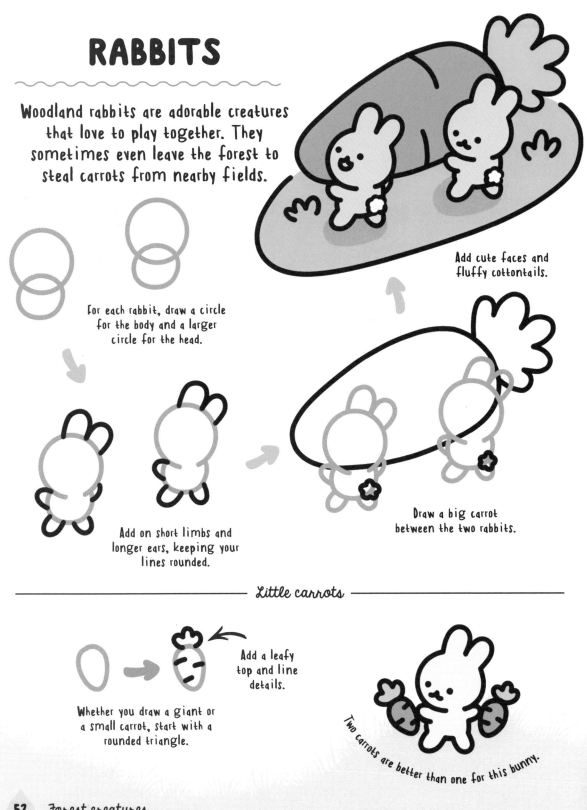

For each rabbit, draw a circle for the body and a larger circle for the head.

Add on short limbs and longer ears, keeping your lines rounded.

Draw a big carrot between the two rabbits.

Add cute faces and fluffy cottontails.

Little carrots

Whether you draw a giant or a small carrot, start with a rounded triangle.

Add a leafy top and line details.

Two carrots are better than one for this bunny.

Catching bugs

Then add on the limbs and ears.

Draw a circle head and gumdrop body.

Give your rabbit a net and some butterflies to chase.

Flower bunny

Draw a circle head and jelly bean body.

Add on the round legs, long ears, and a face.

Add the fluffy cottontail and finish with a flower necklace.

Snoozing bunny

Similar to the body, the mushroom is also an oval shape.

Give the mushroom a stem and a fun pattern.

BIRDS

Lots of birds live in forests, some in the trees and others in bushes or on woodland lakes.

Duck

Start a duck by drawing two ovals and a curved line for the wing.

Add the tail, bill, and eyes, and give your duck a dainty flower hat.

Draw a pond around your duck, and include some floating flowers and petals.

Forest songbirds

The cardinal has a circle head and semicircle body.

Draw a rectangle tail and add triangle features on the head.

A blue jay has a triangle-shaped crest on its head.

Woodpecker

Start with a circle head and egg-shaped body.

Most of the woodpecker's features are triangles.

Give the woodpecker a tree trunk and action markings to show it is pecking for food.

Owl

The base of an owl consists of two ovals and a triangle tail.

Use curved lines to smooth the body out and add facial shaping.

Give your owl a branch to perch on.

In flight

To draw outstretched wings, start with a jelly bean . . .

. . . then add feathers along the outline.

Keep adding feathers to the inside of the jelly bean shape.

Use the same technique to draw the wings flapping back.

Owls like to swoop down to the ground and grab things with their feet. Their feet are very strong and they use them to protect themselves from danger.

CATERPILLARS

Before they turn into butterflies or moths, caterpillars spend much of their time munching on leaves. So why not draw your caterpillar on a leaf, so it has a tasty snack?

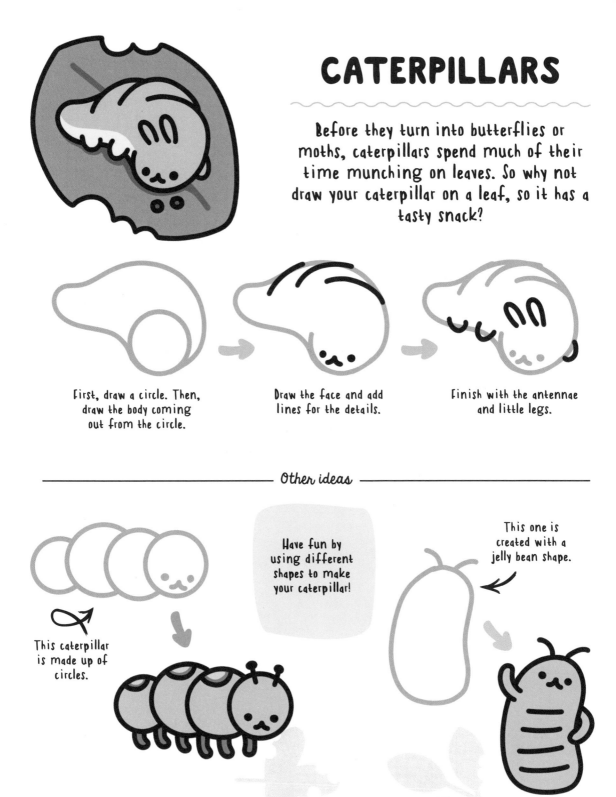

First, draw a circle. Then, draw the body coming out from the circle.

Draw the face and add lines for the details.

Finish with the antennae and little legs.

Other ideas

This caterpillar is made up of circles.

Have fun by using different shapes to make your caterpillar!

This one is created with a jelly bean shape.

BUTTERFLIES AND MOTHS

Butterflies and moths are very similar, but one of the differences is that butterflies hold their wings up, while moths hold their wings closer to their bodies.

Give your butterfly a face and fill out its antennae.

For a butterfly, draw an egg shape for the body, and a double-wing on each side that reaches above and below the body.

Use curved lines to start drawing the wing pattern.

Complete the wing pattern with a few straight lines, and start the antennae.

— Moth wings —

Start with an oval for the body and rectangle legs.

Draw wings that face downward, a bit like dog ears! Draw lines to start the antennae.

Fill out the wings and body, then add a face and round tops on the antennae.

This moth's wings are horizontal, and still in a downward position.

SMALL CRITTERS

Some of the small critters you might find in the forest include cute mice, skunks, and hedgehogs.

Draw a circle for the head and add a curved triangle for the snout.

When coloring a skunk, make the center of the face and tail white. The rest can be colored gray.

Add little ears and facial features.

The body is an oval, the legs are round, and the tail is big and wavy.

!!!

Sitting skunk

Draw a circle head and egg-shaped body.

Add the limbs, head details, and wavy tail.

This skunk let out a scent!

The hedgehog is simple to draw: start with an oval.

Add a rounded triangle snout. The ears and limbs are the same shape.

Draw lots of little lines for the spines.

This hedgehog is about to curl into a ball. Draw a fat jelly bean shape.

Add the face at the top left. The arms are folded so they look like circles.

Hedgehogs like to eat worms and caterpillars.

Add the spines all over the hedgehog's body.

Mouse

A mouse is made of circles and ovals. Its ears are quite large.

Give the mouse a strawberry to hold and a curly tail.

This strawberry looks massive, but actually the mouse is very small.

Small critters 59

RACCOONS

Raccoons are food raiders, and are great at finding things in the wild. Their long claws allow them to hold on to objects, unlike most other animals.

Draw cookie crumbs on the raccoon's face.

I always start my raccoon drawings with two ovals. Then I add on the triangle ears and big tail.

Add a face and draw the hands pointing upward so it can hold the cookie.

Pay attention to the pattern on the raccoon's face and tail.

Don't forget to draw those long nails!

— Sleepy head —

This sleeping raccoon has a large semicircle body and rounded paws reaching forward.

Give the sleepy raccoon a circular, snoring mouth.

Raccoons are also notorious climbers! Draw this one snoozing on a branch. Add some 'Z's to show it's asleep.

SNAKES

Snakes are super-cute reptiles with beady eyes. Their unique body shape means they can take on all manner of poses, plus you can play with the patterns on their skin.

Draw a wide oval head and a long, slithering body, with a pointed end.

Add patterns on the back.

Dot in an eye and give your snake a tongue.

Sitting snakes

If you are experimenting with different body positions for your snake, still start with an oval head.

This wizard snake is casting spells from a magical book!

You can make really unique snake designs inspired by your favorite plants or mushrooms.

To draw a flower crown, start with an oval base.

LADYBUGS

While most ladybugs are red or orange, some types are pink, tan, and even blue. Their spots fool predators into thinking they are poisonous.

Draw a small gumdrop head and two pointy ovals for wings. The wing closest to you is bigger than the back wing.

Add more pointed ovals for the inner wings. Add the antennae and an eye.

Finish by adding spots on the front wings and lines on the inner wings.

Stand up

Start with a small circle for a head and a larger circle for the body.

Add two legs and a triangle shape where the bug's wings meet. Add spots, eyes, and antennae.

You could give your ladybugs some clothes.

The base of a ladybug consists of mostly circles and ovals.

BEES

Bees can be drawn in various ways, with base shapes usually consisting of circles and jelly bean shapes!

Draw a circle head and a jelly bean body.

Draw a wavy shape to give your bee a neck frill. Draw two oval wings and two antennae.

Add four little limbs, a big round eye with a half-moon highlight, and the stripes.

— *Simply stripy* —

You can also draw bees without giving them separate heads.

Draw simple line limbs and antennae. Do in the eyes and add the stripes.

Think of this base as a triangular jelly bean.

Make the wings small and round.

Draw a jellybean and a curved wing.

Add a second wing, stripes, and little limbs. You could even add a honeycomb.

WOLVES

Wolves are depicted as the scary bad guy in fairy tales, but we're here to make them lovable and cute!

Wolves travel together in a pack.

Draw a circle head and jelly bean body!

The wolf is walking forward. Notice how the legs move.

The ears and tail are triangle shaped.

Add more fur details by drawing triangles around the head.

A wolf's face is made up of circles and triangles.

Wolves love to howl at the moon.

Don't forget the ruffly fur.

The seated wolf has a jelly bean body and oval head inside the jelly bean.

Draw rectangles for the front legs.

Sleeping wolf

Draw the front legs extending out and the back legs close to the body.

Draw a rounded snout and spiky fur.

When a wolf is laying down it has a gumdrop body with a circle head inside the body shape.

The ears and fur are the same shape.

Wolves are very similar to dogs. The main differences are their ruffly fur, long noses, and pointy ears.

The fur on the tail also looks spiky.

DEER

Deer are shy creatures, so you'll have to be very quiet if you want to spot one. You can choose to draw your deer with or without antlers.

Start with a circle head and a jelly bean body.

Connect the shapes by drawing the neck. Add curved lines to represent the limbs and snout.

Add rounded ears, a little tail, and facial features.

You can add a spotted pattern on the rump if it is a fawn. Adult deer do not always have spots.

Keeping watch

Add long, rectangular limbs, round ears, and a snout.

Finish off with the pattern details and don't forget to give your deer hooves.

You can give your deer a flower crown.

Antlers

Antlers are simple to draw when you break them down.

Start with a long stick, then keep adding more stick shapes to the sides.

Deer in action

To indicate motion, draw the limbs moving in a particular direction.

Hiking deer

Draw a large circle, a smaller square body, and legs.

Add the head details and the arms, bending the front one at the "elbow."

Give this adventuring deer a cap, walking stick, and backpack.

SNAILS

Snails carry their homes on their backs. They're fun to draw because you can decorate their homes with cool patterns or little trinkets.

The shell is an oval and the body is a rounded triangle.

Fill in the rounded triangle with wavy lines to define the body. Add antennae and a face.

Draw a spiral in the shell, then add the shell pattern. Finish by filling out the antennae.

Try drawing different antennae for each snail. They could be short and stubby or long like bunny ears.

Flower shell

Draw the outline of a flower motif inside the circle shell.

Add two more flower motifs and a pattern on the body too.

Or you could add small flowers to the shell.

Snail trail

Sometimes the shell can be a triangle.

While the body of the snail is the circle.

Give it a trail of plants!

Squashed bodies

You can squash the basic shapes to make a different style of snail.

Shell accessories

You can make the shell a backpack. Give this studious snail a book too!

BEARS

Bears live in forests and grasslands and need a lot of body fat to get them through the hibernating months. Don't be afraid to draw a really round bear!

Give your bear a honeycomb to hold, cute paw details, and a smiling face.

Don't forget the little round ears.

Draw the arms close to the body and the legs pointing outward and flat on the ground.

Start with a large oval head and a smaller gumdrop body.

Your choice of color will distinguish what type of bear you are drawing: perhaps a grizzly bear, black bear, or a panda? Pandas live in bamboo forests.

Teddy bears

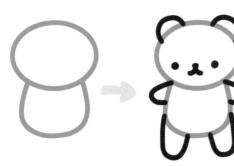

Add legs pointing downward from the bottom of the gumdrop body.

You can give teddy bears character by adding cute outfits.

This bear has an oval head and an egg-shaped body with chubby, short legs.

Draw two rectangles to represent a book, and add the ears and face.

Give your bear a comfy mushroom seat by drawing a large oval and a curved stem.

— Simplified bear —

You can also draw a bear from a single gumdrop.

Simply add a face, ears, and two limbs at the front.

Baby bears can climb on their parents' back when they want to go for a ride. Look at this little one go!

SQUIRRELS

Squirrels can jump more than ten times their length, and use their fluffy tails like parachutes that help them to balance when they leap from tree to tree.

Fill out the tail and finish with an eye and nose.

Start with a round head and oval body.

Add the limbs, snout, and ears. To start the tail, draw a curved line that spirals at the top.

Spiral

One way to draw a spiral is to start with a circle . . .

. . . then draw a curly letter "S" around the circle.

Collecting nuts

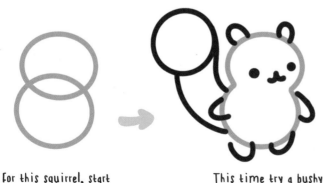

For this squirrel, start with an oval head and a circle body.

This time try a bushy tail. Add short limbs, ears, and a face.

Give your squirrel a sweater and acorn-inspired hat, and a basket to collect nuts in.

Climbing squirrel

Give this squirrel a closed eye, a spiral tail . . .

. . . and a tree to cling on to.

Seated snack

Add short limbs, a little snout, and two small ears.

For a seated squirrel, start with two circles. The head circle is off-center to the body.

Add a spiral tail, a cap and sweater, and a yummy acorn snack!

Sleepy squirrel

Surround your squirrel with acorns and leaves.

This sleepy squirrel has a bushy tail with a circle head and oval body that curve toward the tail.

Give the tail a fluffy feel by adding some loops.

FROGS AND TOADS

Many types of frog live in jungles around the world, and toads like the dank undergrowth of woodland environments. You can make different types of frogs and toads using these simple shapes.

Start by drawing a square.

Draw a jelly bean.

Draw an oval body and a thinner, wider oval head.

Add stubby, round limbs and draw the eyes at the top corners of the square.

Draw the limbs at the bottom of the body.

Add thin limbs and eyes close together on top of the head.

Rain-forest frog

Start with a large oval head and a smaller gumdrop body. Add lines for the limbs.

Put the eyes at the top of the head and fill out the limbs. Give your rain-forest frog a raincoat.

Draw a big leaf for your frog's umbrella.

Stubby toad

Did you know that toads have shorter legs than frogs? Start this toad with a rough semicircle.

Add limbs in front of the body. Dot in the eyes and add a curved line above each eye.

Add a mouth and the toe details.

Floating frog

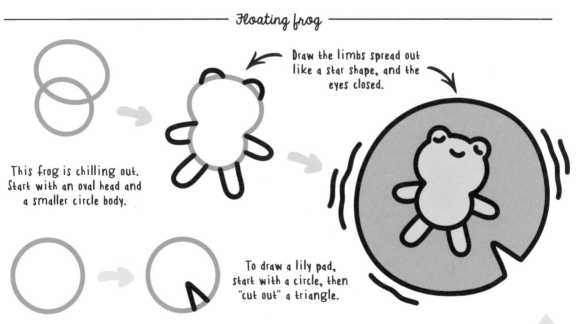

Draw the limbs spread out like a star shape, and the eyes closed.

This frog is chilling out. Start with an oval head and a smaller circle body.

To draw a lily pad, start with a circle, then "cut out" a triangle.

MANTISES

Mantises are insects well known for their folded praying arms, whic is why they are also known as praying mantis.

Draw a tall semicircle for the body, and a wide egg shape for the head. Draw a curved line to begin the top limb and a zigzag for the lower limb.

Fill out the limbs. Add antennae and a wing.

Look at me!

You can use the same shape for the "arms," but draw them outstretched.

Give your mantises clothes to wear, or things to hold.

To draw a mantis with its head facing you, simply adjust the shape of the head.

Draw the eyes sticking out from the sides of the head.

ROLY-POLY BUGS

Roly-poly bugs have a hard outer casing like armor, and can roll up into balls to protect themselves from predators.

Start with a simple jelly bean.

Add in curving horizontal lines and dot in an eye. Add two antennae.

Finish by adding the little legs.

Roll away

Draw an oval with horizontal lines.

Add the legs, antennae, and flowers.

The base of the rolled-up pose is a circle.

When roly-poly bugs curl up into a ball, they can roll around and travel quickly!

NATURE DOGS

Nature dogs have evolved to suit their environment. In winter, nature dogs grow thick fur, while in spring and summer their coats can become flowery or leafy.

Draw a circle for the head and a jelly bean body.

Add the curvy ears and limbs.

Finish with lots of wavy lines for the fuzzy fur.

Seasonal coats

Draw a circle head, an oval body, and a long, thick tail.

Add the curvy ears and just two limbs, plus a fuzzy detail on the head.

With flowers all over its coat, I bet this dog smells lovely!

Start with two ovals for this laying pose.

Draw wavy lines for fur. This time the ears and tail are pointing up.

Add a leafy mustache and leaf details all around.

Rainy-day dog

Draw a circle head and a gumdrop body. Add the limbs.

Just a few lines indicate the pants and jacket. Add the ears.

Draw in some fuzzy details, a useful little bag, and the facial features.

Happy face

Surprised face

You can even have fun dressing your nature dogs, to protect them from the rain or sun.

Forest fashion

Squash up the gumdrop body.

Notice how the back legs point outward.

A few simple lines and dots are all that is needed to indicate the clothes.

Nature dogs

UNICORNS

Unicorns can be quite shy, so forests are great places for them to live.

Add flower decorations too, if you want!

Start with a circle head and a jelly bean body.

When in a jumping pose, the limbs are curved rectangles. Add ears and a nose too.

Draw in the mane, tail, horn, and hoof details, and a smiling face.

— Floral calm —

Make the mane and tail big and bushy looking.

The legs of a seated unicorn are tucked under the body.

Add flowers to the mane and tail, and color them green to look like leaves.

Snacking unicorn

Add rectangular and curved legs to the jelly bean body.

Give this unicorn a full tail and flowers in its mane and in its mouth. Yum!

Out for a stroll

This time draw a triangle body shape, round head, and straight front leg.

Bend the back leg to show the unicorn is walking. Give your character a warm coat and scarf.

Mini unicorn

Add the nose, tail, and a cool outfit.

The ears stick out from the hood.

Draw a big circle and a squashed oval body. Add the little limbs.

DRAGONS

Dragons have evolved over thousands of years to suit their environments. Sometimes their colors help them with camouflage.

Swirly flower horns

Thorny horns

Refine the wing shapes and add the finishing touches.

Connect the head with the body, then add horns, a tail, and two short legs. Draw the outlines for the wings.

Begin with a circle head and a jelly bean body.

— Cozy dragon —

Draw a cozy dragon by giving it a sweater! Add the clothing on top of the jelly bean body.

The tail and wings are similar shapes; they curve upward and look like antlers.

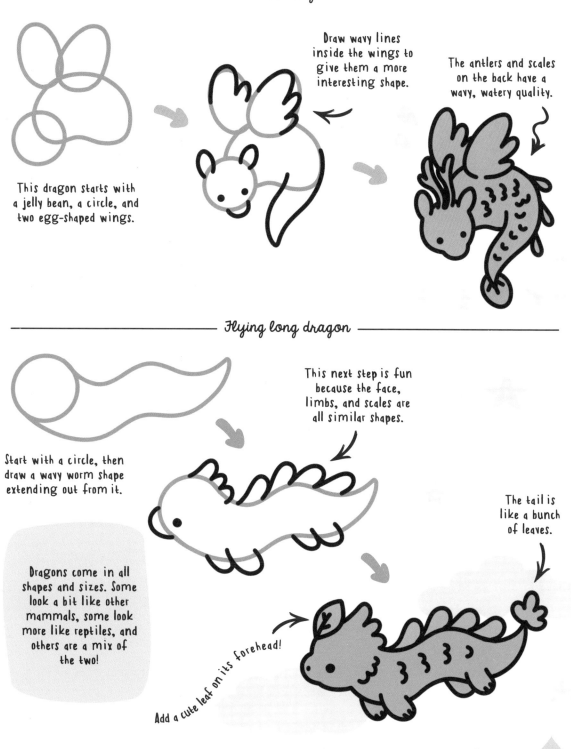

Draw wavy lines inside the wings to give them a more interesting shape.

The antlers and scales on the back have a wavy, watery quality.

This dragon starts with a jelly bean, a circle, and two egg-shaped wings.

Flying long dragon

This next step is fun because the face, limbs, and scales are all similar shapes.

Start with a circle, then draw a wavy worm shape extending out from it.

The tail is like a bunch of leaves.

Dragons come in all shapes and sizes. Some look a bit like other mammals, some look more like reptiles, and others are a mix of the two!

Add a cute leaf on its forehead!

Dragons 83

FUZZY WUZZIES

The fuzzy wuzzy is a sassy, nocturnal, moth-like creature that loves to show off its wings, and is always excited to meet new friends.

Start with a circle head and a gumdrop body.

Draw in the curved limbs and line antennae.

Embellish the antennae with looping lines and draw the face.

Draw heart shapes for the wings and ears.

Add a long tail, a fuzzy body, and a pattern on the wings.

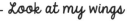 *Look at my wings*

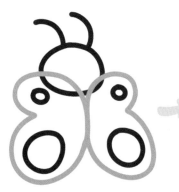

For this pose, start with the wings, which are like squashed heart or jelly bean shapes.

Add a circle head and antennae lines, and large and small circular wing details.

Have fun with the finishing touches.

Play with poses

Add wings, antennae, and limbs to the gumdrop body . . .

Try star-shaped eyes and mouth.

. . . then have fun with different poses and facial expressions.

Tilt the head to show curiosity.

Position the wings downward and add eyebrows for a confident pose.

Sleepy time

A fuzzy wuzzy sleeping on its side starts with a circle for the head and a heart-shaped wing.

Add the second wing, the antennae, and wing details.

Notice how the tail curves inward toward the body.

Fuzzy wuzzies

GROBBLES

Grobbles are mischievous creatures that like to disguise themselves in plant and animal costumes, and play tricks on each other.

The base is made up of circles and round rectangles.

Use wavy lines to draw a plant-inspired hat and neckpiece.

Finish with a face.

Pink and green rose costume

Yellow flower costume

— Sneaky grobble —

The secret to this pose is placing the body to the side of the head, instead of at the center.

Add the ears and limbs and start adding the plant headdress.

Draw big circles for eyes with lines across the top, for that sneaky facial expression.

This line shows the grobble is creeping up on someone.

Flower flying

You can start any grobble with a circle head, gumdrop body, and round limbs.

Add a flower headdress. Draw an oval and a line stem to start the flying flower.

Draw petals in the oval and fill out the stem.

Antler costume

Define the antler shape, and add the finishing touches.

Add antlers to your basic body pose, and a tree-bark costume.

Mushroom costume

Add a big oval on top of the grobble's head, a frilly skirt, and mushroom "maracas."

Give the mushroom headdress a colorful pattern.

SHRUBBIES

These cute little forest creatures can change shape and color depending on their surroundings. They mimic the shapes and shades around them, so they don't stand out.

Start with a shape like a fried egg.

Draw a wavy line along the bottom edge of both shapes.

Fill in the details of the face, ears, and limbs.

Bounce away

Draw a gumdrop with a smaller gumdrop inside for the face.

Add a wavy line along the bottom edge of the body and the face. Draw the ears, arms, and facial details.

Add in long legs and motion lines to show the shrubbie is jumping up.

Spiky shrubbie

This shrubbie is spiky, so add pointy triangles instead of wavy lines to the fried-egg base shape.

Finish off with the face, ears, and limbs.

Boxy shrubbie

Change the position of the facial features to show that this shrubbie is looking to the side.

For a boxy shrubbie, draw square shapes along the edges.

Curly shrubbie

Give this shrubbie a circular mouth to show shock.

The curly shrubbie has fancy loops and curls along the body edge.

Chapter four

THE NATURAL WORLD

In this chapter you will find trees, bushes, acorns, mushrooms, and more! Create a beautiful forest for all your creatures to live in.

MUSHROOMS

Mushrooms are umbrella-shaped fungi, which come in different shapes, colors, and sizes. They can grow from soil or even trees. Some mushrooms are poisonous.

All mushrooms have a stem and a cap. For this type start with a wavy oval shape.

Add a long, thin stem below the cap.

Finish with a cute face on the stem.

Mushrooms make great shapes for hats and dresses. Discover more ways to combine plants with people on pages 40—43.

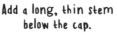

Do you like my outfit? It's mushroom themed!

Some mushrooms have fatter stems and triangular caps.

Draw the cap and stem shapes.

Add little arms and legs to turn your mushroom into a little character.

When you add patterns to your mushroom caps, don't forget that the textures can pop out from the surface.

You can choose to draw a face on the mushroom cap or the body. There's no right or wrong way!

Tree fungi

To draw mushrooms growing out from a tree, start with an oval.

Add a second, tiny mushroom.

Draw curved lines under the cap of the mushroom and thin jelly bean patterns on the cap.

Hats

By drawing a face on the stem of the mushroom, your character instantly gets a cute hat!

Start with a rounded triangle for the hat. Add a square body and rounded limbs.

Give the hat a fun pattern.

This hat is a wide, curvy triangle.

Add a wavy line at the bottom of the triangle. Give your character some arms and legs.

Draw in remaining details like the face and lines on the hat.

Enoki

Enoki mushrooms have unique caps.

Start with a circle body and add limbs.

Draw small clusters of circles above the body.

Add in lines to connect the clusters to the body.

When mushrooms grow in clusters, they emerge from a central point. You can always add more mushrooms to your cluster, just keep drawing them out from the sides.

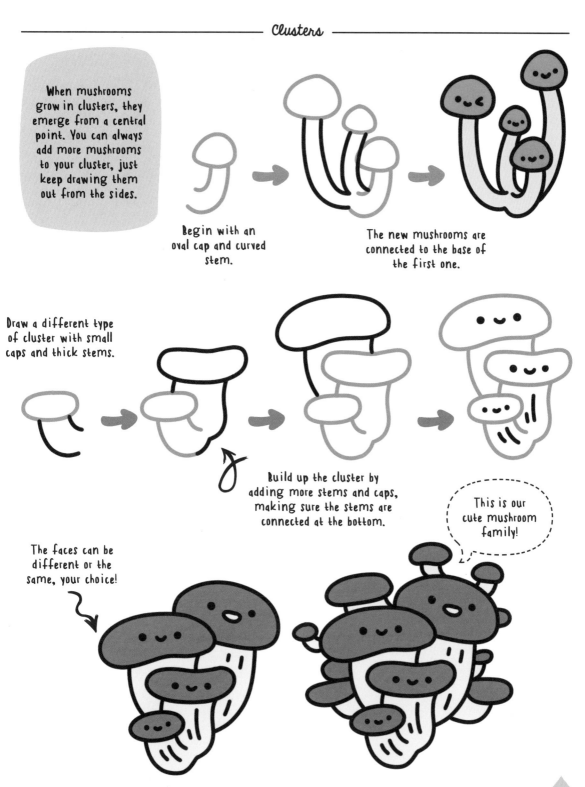

Begin with an oval cap and curved stem.

The new mushrooms are connected to the base of the first one.

Draw a different type of cluster with small caps and thick stems.

Build up the cluster by adding more stems and caps, making sure the stems are connected at the bottom.

This is our cute mushroom family!

The faces can be different or the same, your choice!

VINES

Vines can grow really long, sometimes wrapping up and around trees or other plants, and sometimes hanging down. They can have different types of leaves and even flowers.

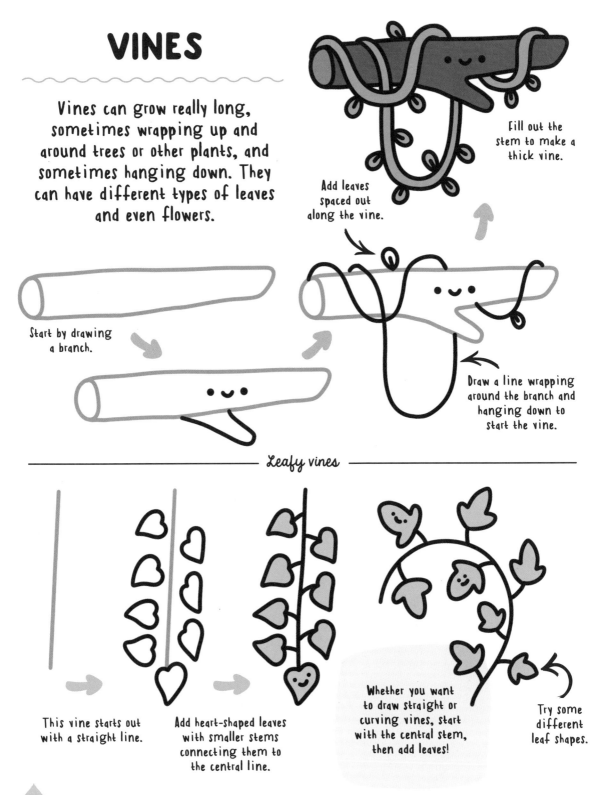

Fill out the stem to make a thick vine.

Add leaves spaced out along the vine.

Start by drawing a branch.

Draw a line wrapping around the branch and hanging down to start the vine.

Leafy vines

This vine starts out with a straight line.

Add heart-shaped leaves with smaller stems connecting them to the central line.

Whether you want to draw straight or curving vines, start with the central stem, then add leaves!

Try some different leaf shapes.

Trailing vines

Vines are popular houseplants. Draw a pot with a few lines for the central stems.

Add leaves and smaller stems. These leaves are rounded triangles.

To add flowers to your vines, draw looping wavy lines down from the stem and back up again.

Hanging vines

Hanging pots are perfect for vine houseplants. Start with a gumdrop.

Draw the stems coming out of the pot and draping downward.

Now add in lots of oval leaves.

Draw the three cords that the pot hangs from.

TREES

When drawing trees, you can always count on the fact that they have a single trunk at the center with leaves coming out from the top. Experiment with different shapes for the treetops and leaves to draw different types of tree.

Draw a rectangle for the trunk and a fluid clump on top.

Draw wavy lines around the top clump to give a natural tree shape.

Add a face and little leaves poking out.

Evergreen

This style of tree has a rectangle trunk and a triangle on top.

Draw a symmetrical shape inside the triangle to make a fir tree.

Draw a bunch of trees in one area to grow a forest.

For this tree, draw an oval on top of the rectangle trunk.

The branches and leaves of a weeping willow hang down from the oval canopy.

Fruit trees

Draw a wavy line around the jelly bean outline and circles for the fruit.

Make this an apple tree by coloring the fruit red and adding a small leaf on each apple.

Draw a large jelly bean and add a "Y"-shaped trunk.

You can use the same base to make different types of trees. A holly tree has spiky leaves and small berries.

Trees 99

FLOWERS

There are so many types of flowers and multiple ways to draw them (as separate flowers or combined bouquets). Here are some of my favorite species, drawn cute!

Start with a big circle. The stem comes out from the center.

Draw long, rounded petals coming out from the circle.

Sunflowers have yellow petals that make them look like the sun. Try drawing a sun with matching yellow rays shining out!

The leaves are heart-shaped.

More flowers

Roses have layered petals, spiky leaves, and thorns on the stem.

Tulips are my all-time favorites: they have oval petals.

Hydrangea have clusters of small petals that look like stars.

Peonies have layered petals like roses, but without the thorns.

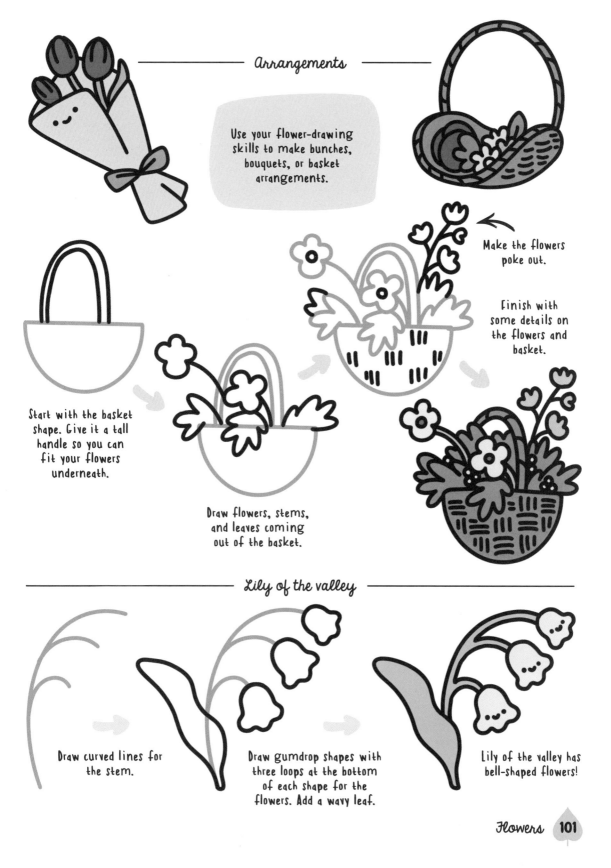

Arrangements

Use your flower-drawing skills to make bunches, bouquets, or basket arrangements.

Start with the basket shape. Give it a tall handle so you can fit your flowers underneath.

Draw flowers, stems, and leaves coming out of the basket.

Make the flowers poke out.

Finish with some details on the flowers and basket.

Lily of the valley

Draw curved lines for the stem.

Draw gumdrop shapes with three loops at the bottom of each shape for the flowers. Add a wavy leaf.

Lily of the valley has bell-shaped flowers!

LEAVES

Leaves are little blades that come in many colors depending on the plant type or season of the year. Here are different shapes to draw.

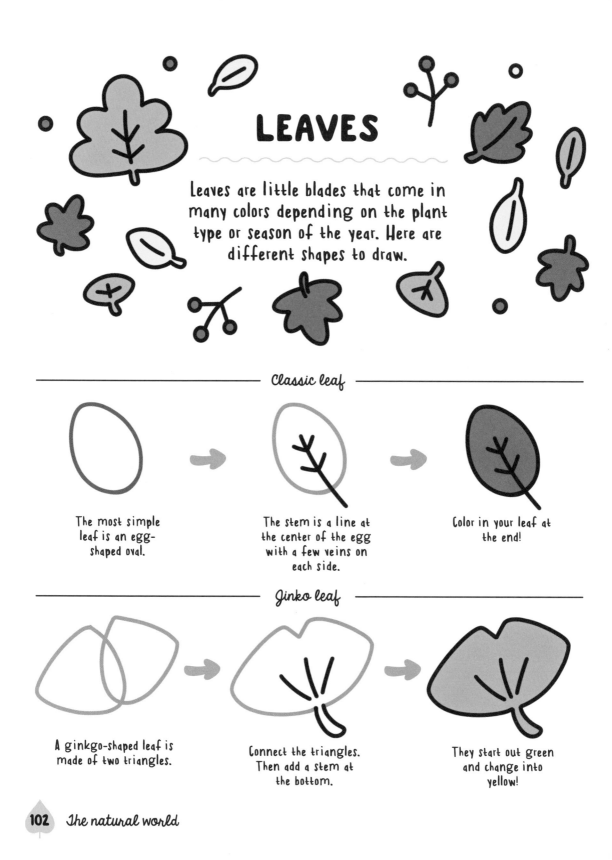

Classic leaf

The most simple leaf is an egg-shaped oval.

The stem is a line at the center of the egg with a few veins on each side.

Color in your leaf at the end!

Ginko leaf

A ginkgo-shaped leaf is made of two triangles.

Connect the triangles. Then add a stem at the bottom.

They start out green and change into yellow!

Maple leaf

Draw three rounded triangles.

Add two more larger triangles at the bottom.

Complete the drawing with a stem.

Poison leaf

Start with two lines that cross each other.

Add the leaves at the end of the lines.

Three leaves usually means it could be poisonous and itchy!

Large leaf

Begin this leaf by drawing three round bumps.

Complete the bottom with four more bumps.

Draw in a line at the center for the stem.

BUSHES

Under the trees in the forest you can also find lots of different plants, including flower and berry bushes.

Give yourself a guideline for drawing strawberry leaves by starting out with a bunch of ovals.

Then draw pointy lines around the circles. This creates the leaf outlines.

Draw some more ovals and stems in between the spaces to create the strawberries.

Add in the details of the strawberries, like the dot seeds and leaves on top.

Add greenery and a pot—your strawberry bush is done!

 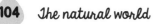

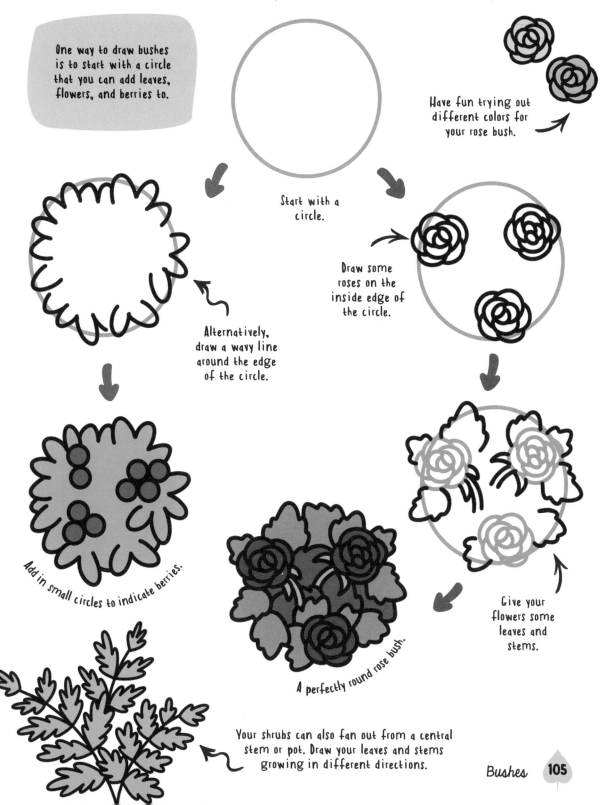

One way to draw bushes is to start with a circle that you can add leaves, flowers, and berries to.

Start with a circle.

Have fun trying out different colors for your rose bush.

Draw some roses on the inside edge of the circle.

Alternatively, draw a wavy line around the edge of the circle.

Add in small circles to indicate berries.

A perfectly round rose bush.

Give your flowers some leaves and stems.

Your shrubs can also fan out from a central stem or pot. Draw your leaves and stems growing in different directions.

Bushes 105

ACORNS, PINE CONES, AND CHESTNUTS

These are the three essential seeds for your woodland world. They are perfect for decorating around your home or making into cute little creatures.

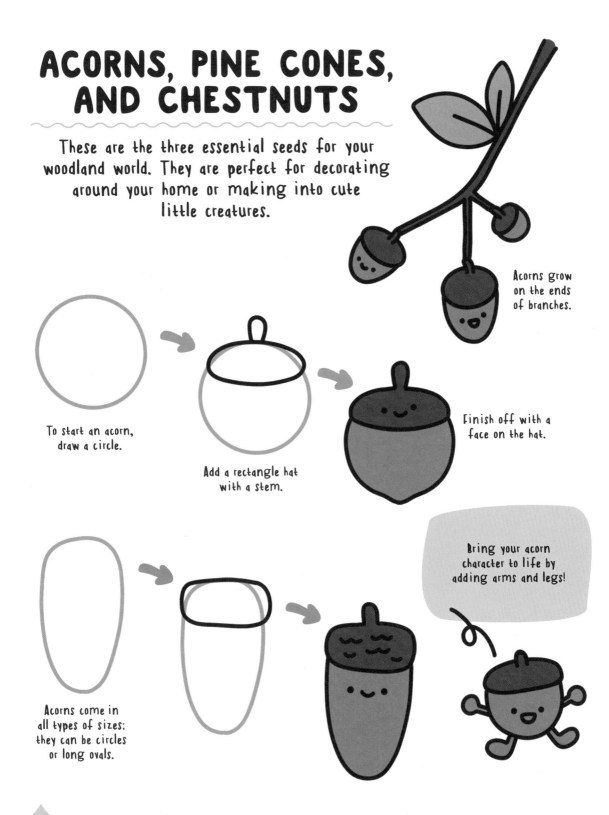

Acorns grow on the ends of branches.

To start an acorn, draw a circle.

Add a rectangle hat with a stem.

Finish off with a face on the hat.

Acorns come in all types of sizes; they can be circles or long ovals.

Bring your acorn character to life by adding arms and legs!

Pine cones assorted with thyme leaves can make cute table decorations. Draw three lines coming out of the pine cones to start the leaves.

I would look great in a wreath! (See page 122.)

Every pine cone starts with an oval.

Draw bumpy lines around the oval to make the pine cone pattern.

Flip the pine cone upside down and add limbs to make a character!

— Chestnuts —

Draw a circle.

Add triangles around the circle.

Chestnuts have a spiky shell.

Keep the mouth close to the eyes to make it even cuter.

Inside the shell is the seed!

MOUNTAINS

Mountains are my favorite scenery type. They are simple to draw because the bases are always made up of triangles, and you can add fun features like trees or water.

Mountains are lighter in color on the top because they usually have snow up there.

Draw two overlapping triangles.

Erase the lines that overlap. Draw in the mountain details like the face and squiggly snow line.

In the clouds

Draw a triangle with rounded corners.

Draw clouds surrounding the mountaintop to show how tall the mountain is.

Draw a wavy line along the base of the mountain, and squiggly shapes for the clouds.

Water on top of mountains comes from melted snow or rain. A pool of water can add a fun element to your mountain drawing.

Draw three overlapping triangles.

Draw an oval for the pool of water and add a waterfall that fills it.

Draw a cloud shape where the falling water crashes into the pool.

Tall and wide

Your mountain could be tall and thin. This one is like a tree, with leaves and branches.

To make your mountain range wide, simply draw more triangles side by side.

ROCKS AND BOULDERS

Something as simple as a rock can be transformed into a super-cute character! With just a face and some added features, you can draw your own rock creatures.

Start with any angular shape that has a top, bottom, and sides.

Now draw straight lines inside the basic shape to make your rock appear three-dimensional.

Add lines that echo the main rock shape.

Finish with a face.

───── Play with shapes ─────

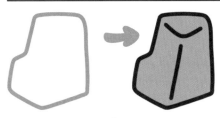

You can transform any two-dimensional shape into a three-dimensional rock . . .

. . . using the same techniques.

Can you make your own rock shapes using these techniques?

Plant rock

Draw the base shape for your rock and add ovals a short distance above.

Use curved lines to connect the ovals to the rock and make mushrooms. Add a wavy line for the moss growing on top of the rock.

Rock creatures

To draw a rock creature, start by drawing the rock base.

Add lines that make up the sides. Then draw the limbs.

The limbs are like smaller rectangle rocks.

This rock creature has a rounded base shape and curved limbs.

Draw a wavy line all around the top of the rock for the moss.

Make your rock creature wave its arms in the air while it is running to show excitement!

Rocks and boulders

111

CRYSTALS

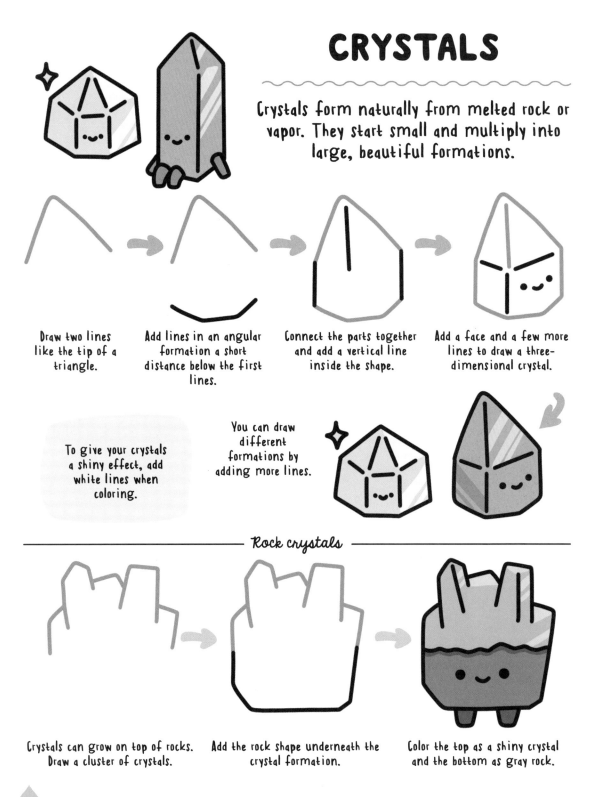

Crystals form naturally from melted rock or vapor. They start small and multiply into large, beautiful formations.

Draw two lines like the tip of a triangle.

Add lines in an angular formation a short distance below the first lines.

Connect the parts together and add a vertical line inside the shape.

Add a face and a few more lines to draw a three-dimensional crystal.

To give your crystals a shiny effect, add white lines when coloring.

You can draw different formations by adding more lines.

Rock crystals

Crystals can grow on top of rocks. Draw a cluster of crystals.

Add the rock shape underneath the crystal formation.

Color the top as a shiny crystal and the bottom as gray rock.

Crystal formations

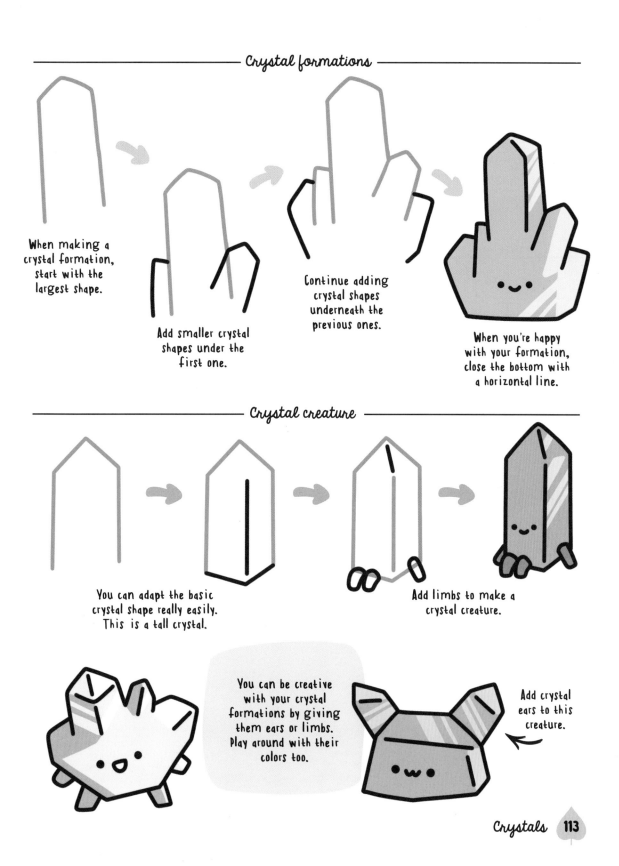

When making a crystal formation, start with the largest shape.

Add smaller crystal shapes under the first one.

Continue adding crystal shapes underneath the previous ones.

When you're happy with your formation, close the bottom with a horizontal line.

Crystal creature

You can adapt the basic crystal shape really easily. This is a tall crystal.

Add limbs to make a crystal creature.

You can be creative with your crystal formations by giving them ears or limbs. Play around with their colors too.

Add crystal ears to this creature.

Chapter five

FOREST LIVING

Everything can be cute! To complete your
woodland world, you need to give a woodland
twist to inanimate objects, from houses to
vehicles and everything in between.

HOMES

When it comes to drawing homes for your woodland folk and forest creatures, you can be really creative. Build homes in the trees, on water, or even out of the natural forest landscape.

This is a mushroom house with lots of extensions! Draw a mushroom base.

Draw circle windows, an arched door, and circles on the roof.

Fill out the log and add mushrooms sprouting out from it.

Draw a circle to indicate the log that the house sits on.

To draw a tree house, start with a tree, then add the house nestled in the branches.

Lily pad home

This house floats on water! Draw a circle for the lily pad, then design a home on top of it.

Show that it's floating with water lines.

Bush garden home

Draw this home if your woodland friends enjoy gardening.

Add a checkered pattern on the roof.

The base of this home is made up of rectangles and triangles.

Fruit home

Create a cute fruit house by drawing the fruit first. Then add a door and windows.

Add grass around the house to complete the scene.

FURNITURE

Fill your forest homes with chic woodland furniture. Here are some pieces that I think you will like.

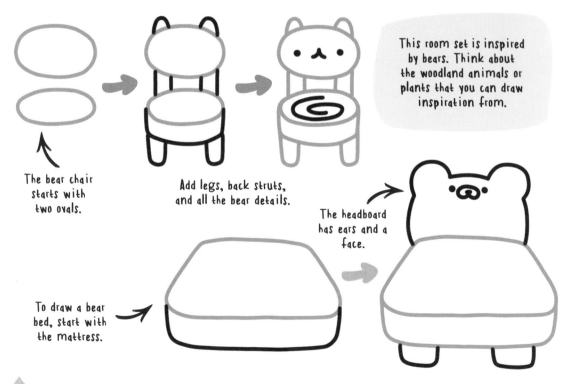

The bear chair starts with two ovals.

Add legs, back struts, and all the bear details.

This room set is inspired by bears. Think about the woodland animals or plants that you can draw inspiration from.

The headboard has ears and a face.

To draw a bear bed, start with the mattress.

Froggy furniture

For a frog chair, draw an oval seat and gumdrop back.

Add some oval arms . . .

. . . and gumdrop legs.

Draw round froggy eyes on top of the chair back.

My favorite frog color is lime green, because it's bright and eye-catching.

Look at this cute little frog sitting on top of a mushroom table!

Use frog characteristics on a bookcase.

Flower lamp

Begin the drawing with an oval at the bottom and lines for stems.

This lamp is inspired by flowers, so the shades are tulips.

Add a friend!

HOUSEPLANTS

Having houseplants is like bringing the forest indoors with you. Plants can brighten up any home, and bring in more oxygen.

Draw a plant pot. This one is like an upside-down gumdrop.

Pilea plants have circle leaves.

Draw circles of different sizes all around the top.

Connect the circles to the pot by drawing stems.

Use different shades of green for the leaves and stems.

The number of leaves that your houseplant has is completely up to you! I keep adding leaves until I feel like my drawing is full.

Leaves on leaves

Sometimes I like to start by drawing leaves instead of the pot.

Keep adding leaves on top of one another.

Add leaf veins. Draw the pot at the bottom and then add a face.

Spiky

The snake plant is a popular houseplant. Start with the pot.

Draw wavy, spiky leaves coming up from the pot.

Add a cute snake face to the pot!

Frilly

Some houseplants have frilly leaves. Draw the leaf shape . . .

. . . then add wavy lines all around.

I have given this plant a stand for the pot to sit on.

Other ideas

If you have houseplants at home, you'll know that they come in lots of shapes and sizes. Try drawing your own houseplants and making them cute.

The monstera has heart-shaped leaves.

Succulents don't need much watering.

Willow-woven baskets can be filled with all sorts of objects.

EVERYDAY OBJECTS

Decorations and accessories inspired by woodland themes are the icing on the cake for your cute character and environment drawings. There are endless possibilities to combine everyday objects with forest themes, and I've given just a few examples here.

Woodland wreath

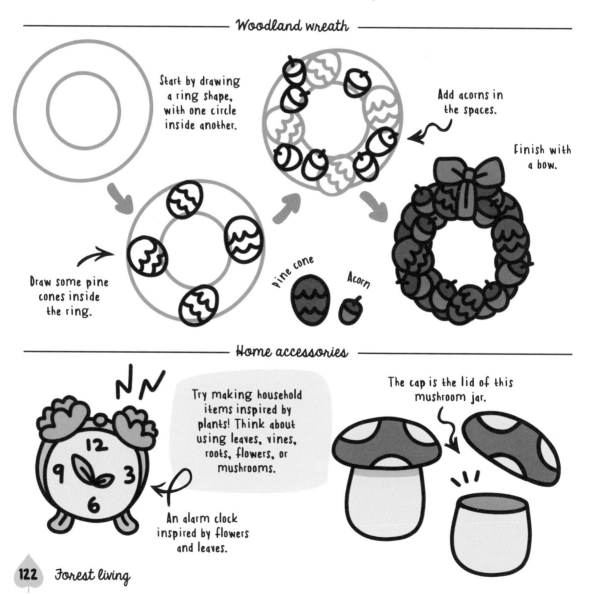

Start by drawing a ring shape, with one circle inside another.

Add acorns in the spaces.

Finish with a bow.

Draw some pine cones inside the ring.

Pine cone

Acorn

Home accessories

Try making household items inspired by plants! Think about using leaves, vines, roots, flowers, or mushrooms.

The cap is the lid of this mushroom jar.

An alarm clock inspired by flowers and leaves.

Character accessories

Draw a gumdrop shape for the base of a bag.

Draw the bag details and add a duck's tail and head shape on each side of the bag.

Add the duck's bill and eye, and a long strap.

On rainy days, give your woodland characters a giant leaf as an umbrella.

Try making a cat bag.

Technology

Technological accessories may seem out of place in a nature-based scene, but even phones, tablets, and game consoles can be transformed using woodland themes.

Draw a game controller, computer, or phone.

Add plants popping out of the screen.

This one is a flip phone!

FOOD AND DRINK

When creating woodland food, think of nature-inspired designs or fresh ingredients that can be found at farmers' markets. You can decorate dishware with plant patterns, or even give your food animal characteristics.

Honey made by forest bees.

Flowers on a teapot.

Nature patterns on the plates.

Lay the table with oval plates. Then start adding the food.

This is a cute teatime scene, with lovely treats. You could add triangle sandwiches or round cookies.

The honey pot has a pretty bow.

This cake has frosting around the edges and strawberries on top.

Have fun adding the foodie details.

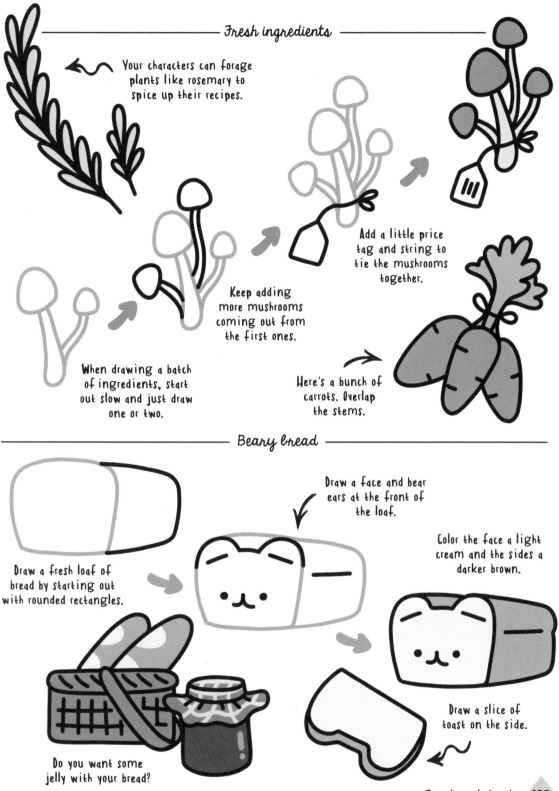

Fresh ingredients

Your characters can forage plants like rosemary to spice up their recipes.

Add a little price tag and string to tie the mushrooms together.

Keep adding more mushrooms coming out from the first ones.

When drawing a batch of ingredients, start out slow and just draw one or two.

Here's a bunch of carrots. Overlap the stems.

Beary bread

Draw a face and bear ears at the front of the loaf.

Color the face a light cream and the sides a darker brown.

Draw a fresh loaf of bread by starting out with rounded rectangles.

Draw a slice of toast on the side.

Do you want some jelly with your bread?

VEHICLES

It is so much fun to make transportation for your characters by combining vehicles with woodland-themed elements.

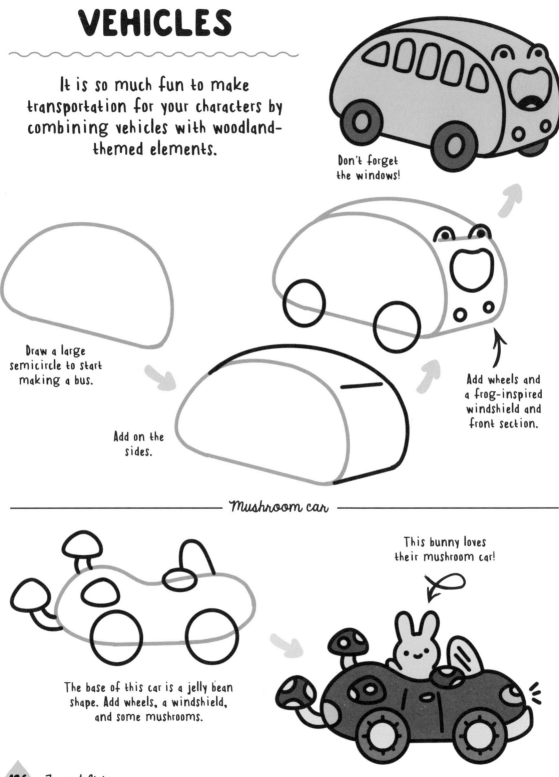

Don't forget the windows!

Draw a large semicircle to start making a bus.

Add on the sides.

Add wheels and a frog-inspired windshield and front section.

— Mushroom car —

The base of this car is a jelly bean shape. Add wheels, a windshield, and some mushrooms.

This bunny loves their mushroom car!

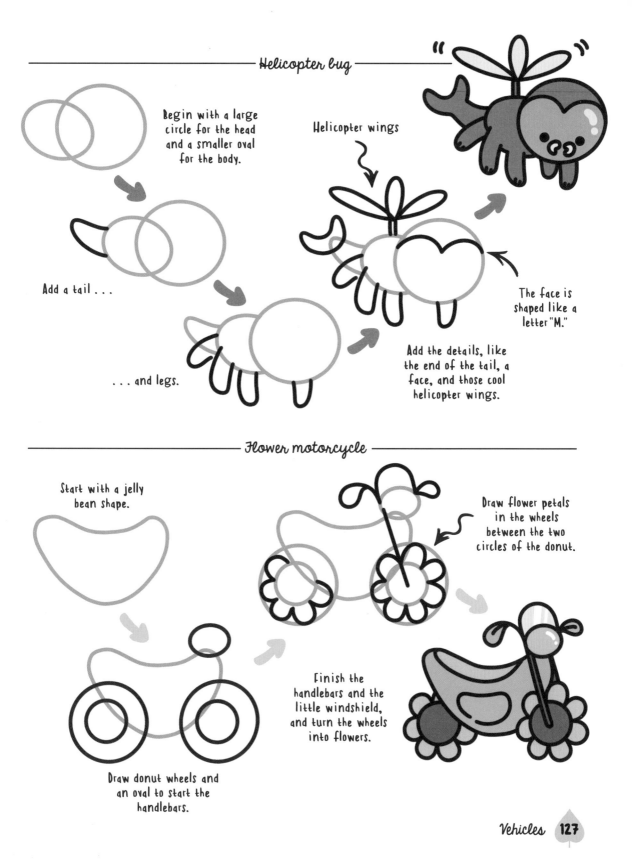

Helicopter bug

Begin with a large circle for the head and a smaller oval for the body.

Add a tail . . .

. . . and legs.

Helicopter wings

The face is shaped like a letter "M."

Add the details, like the end of the tail, a face, and those cool helicopter wings.

Flower motorcycle

Start with a jelly bean shape.

Draw donut wheels and an oval to start the handlebars.

Draw flower petals in the wheels between the two circles of the donut.

Finish the handlebars and the little windshield, and turn the wheels into flowers.

Author Acknowledgments

To the Quarto editing and publishing team, thank you for entertaining my random book ideas and being with me through all of these years. Special shout out to Kate, Claire, Martina, India, and all of the behind-the-scenes team.

Picture Credits

Basileus/Shutterstock.com; ClareM/Shutterstock.com; FineArtSSThai/Shutterstock.com; Fona/Shutterstock.com; Jirawatfoto/Shutterstock.com; KenshiDesign/Shutterstock.com; Mallmo/Shutterstock.com; Martin Spurny/Shutterstock.com; Nai_Pisage/Shutterstock.com; Orientalprincess/Shutterstock.com; Panacea Doll/Shutterstock.com; Puckung/Shutterstock.com; Quayside/Shutterstock.com; r.classen/Shutterstock.com; SpicyTruffel/Shutterstock.com